PILLOW
THOUGHTS

A Journal Approach of Communicating
Between an Adult and a Child

JIM LANDGRAF

authorHOUSE®

AuthorHouse™
1663 Liberty Drive
Bloomington, IN 47403
www.authorhouse.com
Phone: 1 (800) 839-8640

Published by AuthorHouse 09/08/2017

ISBN: 978-1-5462-0735-1 (sc)
ISBN: 978-1-5462-0736-8 (hc)
ISBN: 978-1-5462-0734-4 (e)

Library of Congress Control Number: 2017913757

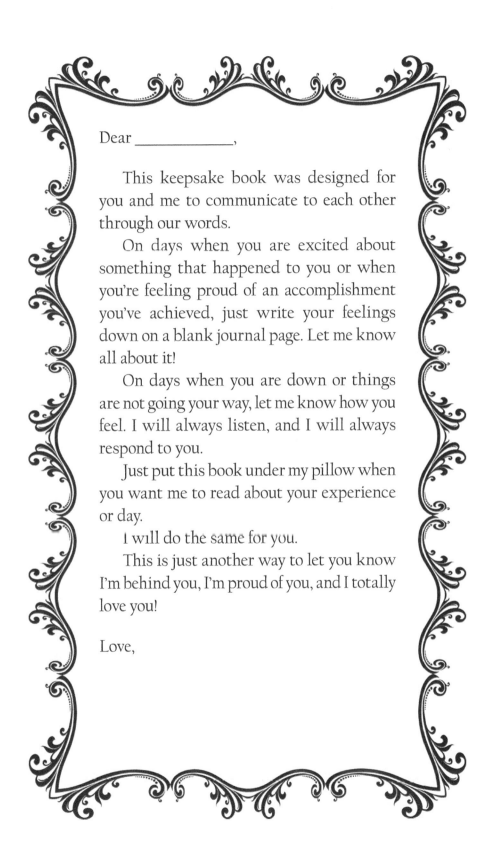

Dear _____,

This keepsake book was designed for you and me to communicate to each other through our words.

On days when you are excited about something that happened to you or when you're feeling proud of an accomplishment you've achieved, just write your feelings down on a blank journal page. Let me know all about it!

On days when you are down or things are not going your way, let me know how you feel. I will always listen, and I will always respond to you.

Just put this book under my pillow when you want me to read about your experience or day.

I will do the same for you.

This is just another way to let you know I'm behind you, I'm proud of you, and I totally love you!

Love,

To my mom, Rose Landgraf, who instilled in me the value of communicating my thoughts and feelings to others on paper

Preface

When I was a young boy, my mother was the sole provider for her nine children. To support her family, she was forced to go back to work full-time. Mom was a registered nurse who found employment at a local nursing home working the night shift. She spent many nights away from my siblings and me, and that meant I didn't have the chance to tell her about my day or how I was feeling about any given topic. During this time, I began to jot down notes to her and slip them under her pillow to read when she came home from work later that night. The following day, I would sometimes find a note under my pillow before I went to sleep. Hence *Pillow Thoughts* got its name, and the idea flourished into this journal today.

I began using *Pillow Thoughts* with my boys when they were in elementary school. The practice of writing and exchanging messages continues even into their adult lives. I feel it helps strengthen my bond with my sons as much as possible. It allows them to write freely concerning their exact feelings without the awkwardness of delving into uncomfortable, personal issues out loud. Over the years, my sons have written to me about growing up and puberty, relationships and girlfriends, and so many other experiences and challenges. These notes have forged a bond between us based on trust and confidentiality. Writing down our thoughts instead of voicing them has been in many ways an easier form of communication for my boys and me. I imagine other people who are striving to have a healthy, communicative relationship with their children may feel the same way. Writing can be a constructive way to focus our feelings. What is written in the journal is never shared with others, unless it is the wish of the person writing.

Pillow Thoughts has proven to be a productive and positive way to communicate with my sons, and I look forward to the day they pass on this tradition to their children.

Twenty-Five Ways to Share Pillow Thoughts

1. Attach a picture of the two of you inside the front cover.
2. Glue in clippings or pictures of events, along with nice messages about the pictures.
3. Write a birthday or holiday message, and include a drawing if you like.
4. Draw a symbol of something that reminds you of each other, and write about it.
5. Offer congratulations on an accomplishment.
6. Write down encouragement in anticipation of a big day.
7. Reaffirm your love to each other when you are disappointed by an action.
8. Reach out when you sense something is on the other person's mind.
9. Express your pride when a goal or milestone is attained or when a defining moment arrives.
10. Mention a funny or sweet remark.
11. Write about overcoming a fear.
12. Praise the mastery of a new skill.
13. Make note of any "firsts," such riding a bike or starting school or a new job.
14. Notice an act of kindness.

15. Rejoice over a moment shared between just the two of you.
16. Share dreams for the future.
17. Define moments of your own guilt or failure.
18. Explain moments of heartbreak.
19. List and share your favorites (food, character, or book, for example) and have the other person share favorites in return.
20. Recollect a favorite moment from the day.
21. Write about "A day in the life of ..." (Parents should complete this type of entry on occasion to show the child's typical day as he or she grows. Include pictures.)
22. Include a guest journal entry. Or, have the child to write a post for his or her future self to read as an adult, sealed in an envelope.
23. Share a poem or story that you think might have meaning for the other person.
24. Express a note that starts, "Read when you need ..." Fill in the blank with love, support, encouragement, or laughter.
25. Mention moments that made you proud or ones that that made your heart melt.

Be creative with your entries. Make them as simple or as complex as you want. But mostly, have fun communicating with each other. Here's a sample to get you started.

Date _____,

Date _____,

_____

_____

_____

_____

_____

_____

_____

_____

_____

_____

_____

_____

_____

_____

Date _____,

_____

_____

_____

_____

_____

_____

_____

_____

_____

_____

_____

_____

_____

_____

_____

Date _____,

_____

_____

_____

_____

_____

_____

_____

_____

_____

_____

_____

_____

_____

_____

Date _____,

_____

_____

_____

_____

_____

_____

_____

_____

_____

_____

_____

_____

_____

_____

_____

_____

Date _____,

_____

_____

_____

_____

_____

_____

_____

_____

_____

_____

_____

_____

_____

_____

_____

Date _____,

_____

_____

_____

_____

_____

_____

_____

_____

_____

_____

_____

_____

_____

_____

_____

Date _____,

_____

_____

_____

_____

_____

_____

_____

_____

_____

_____

_____

_____

_____

_____

Date _____,

_____

_____

_____

_____

_____

_____

_____

_____

_____

_____

_____

_____

_____

_____

_____

Date _____,

_____

_____

_____

_____

_____

_____

_____

_____

_____

_____

_____

_____

_____

_____

_____

Date _____,

Date _____,

_____

_____

_____

_____

_____

_____

_____

_____

_____

_____

_____

_____

_____

_____

_____

_____

Date _____,

_____

_____

_____

_____

_____

_____

_____

_____

_____

_____

_____

_____

_____

_____

_____

_____

Date _____,

_____

_____

_____

_____

_____

_____

_____

_____

_____

_____

_____

_____

_____

_____

_____

Date _____,

Date _____,

Date _____,

23

Date _____,

_____

_____

_____

_____

_____

_____

_____

_____

_____

_____

_____

_____

_____

_____

Date _____,

_____

_____

_____

_____

_____

_____

_____

_____

_____

_____

_____

_____

_____

_____

_____

Date _____,

_____

_____

_____

_____

_____

_____

_____

_____

_____

_____

_____

_____

_____

_____

_____

Date _____,

Date _____,

_____

_____

_____

_____

_____

_____

_____

_____

_____

_____

_____

_____

_____

_____

_____

Date _____,

Date _____,

_____

_____

_____

_____

_____

_____

_____

_____

_____

_____

_____

_____

_____

_____

_____

Date _____,

_____

_____

_____

_____

_____

_____

_____

_____

_____

_____

_____

_____

_____

_____

_____

Date _____,

_____

_____

_____

_____

_____

_____

_____

_____

_____

_____

_____

_____

_____

_____

_____

Date _____ ,

Date _____,

_____

_____

_____

_____

_____

_____

_____

_____

_____

_____

_____

_____

_____

_____

_____

_____

Date _____,

_____

_____

_____

_____

_____

_____

_____

_____

_____

_____

_____

_____

_____

_____

_____

Date _____,

_____

_____

_____

_____

_____

_____

_____

_____

_____

_____

_____

_____

_____

_____

_____

_____

Date _____ ,

_____

_____

_____

_____

_____

_____

_____

_____

_____

_____

_____

_____

_____

_____

_____

_____

Date _____,

_____

_____

_____

_____

_____

_____

_____

_____

_____

_____

_____

_____

_____

_____

_____

Date _____,

_____

_____

_____

_____

_____

_____

_____

_____

_____

_____

_____

_____

_____

_____

Date _____,

Date _____ ,

41

Date _____,

_____
_____
_____
_____
_____
_____
_____
_____
_____
_____
_____
_____
_____
_____
_____
_____

Date _____,

_____

_____

_____

_____

_____

_____

_____

_____

_____

_____

_____

_____

_____

_____

_____

Date _____,

Date _____,

Date _____,

_____

_____

_____

_____

_____

_____

_____

_____

_____

_____

_____

_____

_____

_____

_____

Date _____,

_____

_____

_____

_____

_____

_____

_____

_____

_____

_____

_____

_____

_____

_____

_____

_____

Date _____,

_____

_____

_____

_____

_____

_____

_____

_____

_____

_____

_____

_____

_____

_____

_____

_____

Date _____,

Date _____,

_____

_____

_____

_____

_____

_____

_____

_____

_____

_____

_____

_____

_____

_____

Date _____,

Date _____,

_____

_____

_____

_____

_____

_____

_____

_____

_____

_____

_____

_____

_____

_____

_____

Date _____,

Date _____,

_____

_____

_____

_____

_____

_____

_____

_____

_____

_____

_____

_____

_____

_____

_____

Date _____,

_____

_____

_____

_____

_____

_____

_____

_____

_____

_____

_____

_____

_____

_____

_____

_____

Date _____,

_____

_____

_____

_____

_____

_____

_____

_____

_____

_____

_____

_____

_____

Date _____,

Date _____,

_____

_____

_____

_____

_____

_____

_____

_____

_____

_____

_____

_____

_____

_____

_____

Date _____,

_____

_____

_____

_____

_____

_____

_____

_____

_____

_____

_____

_____

_____

_____

_____

Date _____,

_____

_____

_____

_____

_____

_____

_____

_____

_____

_____

_____

_____

_____

_____

Date _____,

Date _____,

_____

_____

_____

_____

_____

_____

_____

_____

_____

_____

_____

_____

_____

_____

Date _____,

_____

_____

_____

_____

_____

_____

_____

_____

_____

_____

_____

_____

_____

_____

_____

_____

_____

Date _____,

Date _____,

_____

_____

_____

_____

_____

_____

_____

_____

_____

_____

_____

_____

_____

_____

_____

Date _____,

_____

_____

_____

_____

_____

_____

_____

_____

_____

_____

_____

_____

_____

_____

Date _____,

67

Date _____,

_____

_____

_____

_____

_____

_____

_____

_____

_____

_____

_____

_____

_____

_____

Date _____,

Date _____,

70

Date _____,

_____

_____

_____

_____

_____

_____

_____

_____

_____

_____

_____

_____

_____

_____

Date _____,

_____

_____

_____

_____

_____

_____

_____

_____

_____

_____

_____

_____

_____

_____

_____

Date _____,

_____

_____

_____

_____

_____

_____

_____

_____

_____

_____

_____

_____

_____

_____

_____

_____

Date _____,

_____

_____

_____

_____

_____

_____

_____

_____

_____

_____

_____

_____

_____

_____

_____

Date _____,

_____

_____

_____

_____

_____

_____

_____

_____

_____

_____

_____

_____

_____

_____

_____

Date _____,

_____

_____

_____

_____

_____

_____

_____

_____

_____

_____

_____

_____

_____

_____

Date _____,

_____

_____

_____

_____

_____

_____

_____

_____

_____

_____

_____

_____

_____

_____

_____

Date _____,

_____

_____

_____

_____

_____

_____

_____

_____

_____

_____

_____

_____

_____

_____

_____

Date _____,

Date _____,

_____

_____

_____

_____

_____

_____

_____

_____

_____

_____

_____

_____

_____

_____

Date _____,

_____

_____

_____

_____

_____

_____

_____

_____

_____

_____

_____

_____

_____

_____

_____

Date _____,

_____
_____
_____
_____
_____
_____
_____
_____
_____
_____
_____
_____
_____
_____
_____

Date _____,

Date _____,

_____

_____

_____

_____

_____

_____

_____

_____

_____

_____

_____

_____

_____

_____

Date _____,

Date _____,

_____

_____

_____

_____

_____

_____

_____

_____

_____

_____

_____

_____

_____

_____

Date _____,

Date _____,

Date _____,

_____

_____

_____

_____

_____

_____

_____

_____

_____

_____

_____

_____

_____

_____

_____

_____

Date _____,

_____

_____

_____

_____

_____

_____

_____

_____

_____

_____

_____

_____

_____

_____

_____

Date _____,

Date _____,

_____

_____

_____

_____

_____

_____

_____

_____

_____

_____

_____

_____

_____

_____

_____

Date _____,

Date _____,

_____

_____

_____

_____

_____

_____

_____

_____

_____

_____

_____

_____

_____

_____

_____

Date _____,

Date _____,

_____

_____

_____

_____

_____

_____

_____

_____

_____

_____

_____

_____

_____

_____

_____

Date _____,

Date _____,

_____

_____

_____

_____

_____

_____

_____

_____

_____

_____

_____

_____

_____

_____

Date _____,

Date _____,

Date _____,

Date _____,

Date _____,

_____

_____

_____

_____

_____

_____

_____

_____

_____

_____

_____

_____

_____

_____

_____

_____

Date _____,

_____

_____

_____

_____

_____

_____

_____

_____

_____

_____

_____

_____

_____

_____

_____

Date _____,

Date _____,

_____

_____

_____

_____

_____

_____

_____

_____

_____

_____

_____

_____

_____

_____

_____

Date _____,

Date _____,

_____

_____

_____

_____

_____

_____

_____

_____

_____

_____

_____

_____

_____

_____

_____

Date _____,

109

Date _____,

_____

_____

_____

_____

_____

_____

_____

_____

_____

_____

_____

_____

_____

_____

Date _____ ,

_____

_____

_____

_____

_____

_____

_____

_____

_____

_____

_____

_____

_____

_____

_____

_____

Date _____,

_____

_____

_____

_____

_____

_____

_____

_____

_____

_____

_____

_____

_____

_____

Date _____,

_____

_____

_____

_____

_____

_____

_____

_____

_____

_____

_____

_____

_____

_____

_____

_____

Date _____,

_____

_____

_____

_____

_____

_____

_____

_____

_____

_____

_____

_____

_____

_____

_____

Date _____,

_____

_____

_____

_____

_____

_____

_____

_____

_____

_____

_____

_____

_____

_____

_____

_____

Date _____,

_____

_____

_____

_____

_____

_____

_____

_____

_____

_____

_____

_____

_____

_____

Date _____,

Date _____,

_____

_____

_____

_____

_____

_____

_____

_____

_____

_____

_____

_____

_____

_____

Date _____,

Date _____,

_____

_____

_____

_____

_____

_____

_____

_____

_____

_____

_____

_____

_____

_____

_____

_____

Date _____,

Date _____,

_____

_____

_____

_____

_____

_____

_____

_____

_____

_____

_____

_____

_____

_____

_____

Date _____,

Date _____,

Date _____,

Date _____,

Date _____,

_____

_____

_____

_____

_____

_____

_____

_____

_____

_____

_____

_____

_____

_____

_____

Date _____,

_____

_____

_____

_____

_____

_____

_____

_____

_____

_____

_____

_____

_____

_____

_____

_____

Date _____,

Date _____,

_____

_____

_____

_____

_____

_____

_____

_____

_____

_____

_____

_____

_____

_____

Date _____,

131

Date _____,

_____

_____

_____

_____

_____

_____

_____

_____

_____

_____

_____

_____

_____

_____

Date _____,

Date _____,

_____

_____

_____

_____

_____

_____

_____

_____

_____

_____

_____

_____

_____

_____

Date _____,

Date _____,

_____

_____

_____

_____

_____

_____

_____

_____

_____

_____

_____

_____

_____

_____

Date _____,

Date _____,

_____

_____

_____

_____

_____

_____

_____

_____

_____

_____

_____

_____

_____

_____

_____

Date _____,

_____

_____

_____

_____

_____

_____

_____

_____

_____

_____

_____

_____

_____

_____

_____

_____

Date _____,

_____

_____

_____

_____

_____

_____

_____

_____

_____

_____

_____

_____

_____

_____

_____

Date _____,

Date _____,

_____

_____

_____

_____

_____

_____

_____

_____

_____

_____

_____

_____

_____

_____

Date _____,

Date _____,

_____

_____

_____

_____

_____

_____

_____

_____

_____

_____

_____

_____

_____

_____

Date _____,

_____

_____

_____

_____

_____

_____

_____

_____

_____

_____

_____

_____

_____

_____

_____

_____

Date _____,

_____

_____

_____

_____

_____

_____

_____

_____

_____

_____

_____

_____

_____

_____

Date _____,

Date _____,

_____

_____

_____

_____

_____

_____

_____

_____

_____

_____

_____

_____

_____

_____

Date _____,

_____

_____

_____

_____

_____

_____

_____

_____

_____

_____

_____

_____

_____

_____

_____

_____

Date _____,

_____

_____

_____

_____

_____

_____

_____

_____

_____

_____

_____

_____

_____

_____

Date _____ ,

Date _____,

Date _____,

Date _____,

Date _____,

Date _____,

_____

_____

_____

_____

_____

_____

_____

_____

_____

_____

_____

_____

_____

_____

Date _____,

Date _____,

_____

_____

_____

_____

_____

_____

_____

_____

_____

_____

_____

_____

_____

_____

Date _____,

Date _____,

_____

_____

_____

_____

_____

_____

_____

_____

_____

_____

_____

_____

_____

_____

Date _____,

Date _____,

_____

_____

_____

_____

_____

_____

_____

_____

_____

_____

_____

_____

_____

_____

Date _____,

_____

_____

_____

_____

_____

_____

_____

_____

_____

_____

_____

_____

_____

_____

_____

Date _____,

Date _____,

_____

_____

_____

_____

_____

_____

_____

_____

_____

_____

_____

_____

_____

_____

_____

_____

Date _____,

Date _____,

_____

_____

_____

_____

_____

_____

_____

_____

_____

_____

_____

_____

_____

_____

_____

_____

_____

Date _____,

_____

_____

_____

_____

_____

_____

_____

_____

_____

_____

_____

_____

_____

_____

_____

Date _____,

169

Date _____,

_____

_____

_____

_____

_____

_____

_____

_____

_____

_____

_____

_____

_____

_____

Date _____,

Date _____,

_____

_____

_____

_____

_____

_____

_____

_____

_____

_____

_____

_____

_____

_____

_____

Date _____,

Date _____,

174

Date _____,

_____

_____

_____

_____

_____

_____

_____

_____

_____

_____

_____

_____

_____

_____

_____

Date _____,

_____

_____

_____

_____

_____

_____

_____

_____

_____

_____

_____

_____

_____

_____

Date _____,

_____

_____

_____

_____

_____

_____

_____

_____

_____

_____

_____

_____

_____

_____

_____

_____

Date _____,

Date _____,

_____

_____

_____

_____

_____

_____

_____

_____

_____

_____

_____

_____

_____

_____

_____

Date _____,

Date _____,

Date _____,

_____

_____

_____

_____

_____

_____

_____

_____

_____

_____

_____

_____

_____

_____

Date _____,

_____

_____

_____

_____

_____

_____

_____

_____

_____

_____

_____

_____

_____

_____

_____

_____

Date _____,

_____

_____

_____

_____

_____

_____

_____

_____

_____

_____

_____

_____

_____

_____

Date _____,

_____

_____

_____

_____

_____

_____

_____

_____

_____

_____

_____

_____

_____

_____

_____

_____

Date _____,

_____

_____

_____

_____

_____

_____

_____

_____

_____

_____

_____

_____

_____

_____

_____

Date _____,

_____

_____

_____

_____

_____

_____

_____

_____

_____

_____

_____

_____

_____

_____

_____

Date _____,

_____

_____

_____

_____

_____

_____

_____

_____

_____

_____

_____

_____

_____

_____

Date _____,

Date _____,

Date _____,

_____

_____

_____

_____

_____

_____

_____

_____

_____

_____

_____

_____

_____

_____

Date _____,

Date _____,

_____

_____

_____

_____

_____

_____

_____

_____

_____

_____

_____

_____

_____

Date _____,

_____

_____

_____

_____

_____

_____

_____

_____

_____

_____

_____

_____

_____

_____

_____

_____

Date _____,

_____

_____

_____

_____

_____

_____

_____

_____

_____

_____

_____

_____

_____

_____

_____

Date _____,

_____

_____

_____

_____

_____

_____

_____

_____

_____

_____

_____

_____

_____

_____

_____

Date _____,

Date _____,

_____

_____

_____

_____

_____

_____

_____

_____

_____

_____

_____

_____

_____

_____

_____

Date _____ ,

Date _____,

_____

_____

_____

_____

_____

_____

_____

_____

_____

_____

_____

_____

_____

_____

Date _____,

_____

_____

_____

_____

_____

_____

_____

_____

_____

_____

_____

_____

_____

_____

_____

_____

Date _____,

_____

_____

_____

_____

_____

_____

_____

_____

_____

_____

_____

_____

_____

_____

Date _____,

Date _____,

Date _____,

Date _____,

_____

_____

_____

_____

_____

_____

_____

_____

_____

_____

_____

_____

_____

_____

Date _____,

Date _____,

Date _____,

Date _____,

Date _____,

_____

_____

_____

_____

_____

_____

_____

_____

_____

_____

_____

_____

_____

_____

_____

_____

Date _____,

Date _____,

_____

_____

_____

_____

_____

_____

_____

_____

_____

_____

_____

_____

_____

_____

_____

_____

Date _____,

Date _____,

_____

_____

_____

_____

_____

_____

_____

_____

_____

_____

_____

_____

_____

_____

_____

Date _____,

Date _____,

_____

_____

_____

_____

_____

_____

_____

_____

_____

_____

_____

_____

_____

_____

_____

_____

Date _____,

_____

_____

_____

_____

_____

_____

_____

_____

_____

_____

_____

_____

_____

_____

_____

Date _____,

Date _____,

Date _____,

_____

_____

_____

_____

_____

_____

_____

_____

_____

_____

_____

_____

_____

_____

_____

_____

_____

_____

Date _____,

Date _____,

Date _____,

Date _____,

Date _____,

Date _____,

_____

_____

_____

_____

_____

_____

_____

_____

_____

_____

_____

_____

_____

_____

_____

_____

_____

Date _____,

_____

_____

_____

_____

_____

_____

_____

_____

_____

_____

_____

_____

_____

_____

Date _____,

_____

_____

_____

_____

_____

_____

_____

_____

_____

_____

_____

_____

_____

_____

_____

_____

Date _____,

_____

_____

_____

_____

_____

_____

_____

_____

_____

_____

_____

_____

_____

_____

_____

Date _____,

_____

_____

_____

_____

_____

_____

_____

_____

_____

_____

_____

_____

_____

_____

_____

The Benefits of Writing
in a Journal

As parents, we all know children grow up way too fast. Before we know it, they have surpassed crawling and started running and gone from cooing to nonstop talking. They're in primary school one day and then on to high school the next, and suddenly it's off to college. Eighteen years of "molding" our children goes by in a flash. Thanks to the new digital age, we are able to capture every minute of it on a device that fits into our back pocket, but while pictures and videos are precious timepieces to have, they can't always capture the *heart*, the endearing and overwhelming amount of love from the parent behind the camera. Pen-and paper-journal writing offers an in depth look into one's soul, a true connection to another being. While it may not be as up-to-date and modern as texting, a journal—and especially this journal—is a time capsule that can be passed down through the generations and cherished forever, regardless of changing technology. It's a lifetime in book form.

Journaling is far from a new practice. Journals have been around for ages as a form of almost self-therapy—a way to review events and feelings from one's life while being able to keep the information private. Benefits from keeping a journal include helping to improve your mood by prioritizing your goals and desires and minimizing your fears and anxieties. While journaling is often thought of as something we do for ourselves, something to keep private—burn it before anyone else sees it!—journals can also serve as a great communication tool and a lasting memory book for you and your child.

Presidents have maintained their private journals for posterity; other famous figures have done so for their own purposes. Oscar Wilde, a nineteenth-century playwright, said, "I never travel without my diary. One should always have something sensational to read on the train." It is through the writings of Anne Frank in her journal that many readers worldwide learn about the struggles she personally endured during World War II as a hidden fugitive and then a young teen who was persecuted by the Nazis. She wrote, "I want to write, but more than that, I want to bring out all kinds of things that lie buried deep in my heart."

There is increasing evidence to support the notion that journaling has a positive impact on physical well-being. According to the psychotherapist Maud Purcell, scientific evidence supports that journaling provides other unexpected benefits. The act of writing accesses your left brain, which is analytical and rational. While your left-brain is occupied, your right brain is free to create, intuit, and feel. In sum, writing removes mental blocks and allows you to use all of your brainpower to better understand yourself, others, and the world around you. As you journal, you may begin to experience these benefits:

- clarification of your thoughts and feelings;
- better self-knowledge;
- reduction of stress;
- ability to solve problems more effectively;
- ability to resolve disagreements with others.

I hope you will benefit from sharing *Pillow Thoughts* and this journal becomes a treasured keepsake.

About the Author

Born and raised in Madison, Wisconsin, Jim now lives in Kenosha with his wife, Kathy. Together they have raised four boys to adulthood. Jim is a middle school math teacher who loves to be the center of attention in his classroom. When he is not teaching, Jim enjoys spending time with his wife and boys. He is an active member of his church and freely volunteers time there and in his community in various capacities. After his parents' divorce when he was in fourth grade, Jim became particularly close with his mom. It was then that he began his "pillow thoughts" note writing.